Documents for Democracy

Building America and Literacy Skills Through Primary Sources

Volume 2: 19th Century

**Prepared by
Veronica Burchard
Illustrations by Courtney Burrough**

*Dedicated to my loving husband,
Kyle Burchard,
as well as my mentor and friend,
Claire McCaffery Griffin*

―――――――――――――――――

Unless otherwise noted, no part of this publication may be reproduced, stored, sourced off for use in other publications, or transmitted, in any form or by any means, electronic, mechanical, photocopying, recording or otherwise, without the prior written permission of the American Institute for History Education.

Edited by Matthew F. Galella
Design and typography by Graham Communications

Copyright © 2010 American Institute for History Education
All rights reserved

ISBN-13: 978-0-9826244-1-8

Printed in the United States of America
February 2010

Visit **www.aihe-bookstore.com**

Table of Contents

Self-Reliance 3
- Activating Prior Knowledge 5
- Wrap-up Discussion Questions 14
- Teaching Suggestions 15
- Graphic Organizer A 16
- Handout B 17
- Handout C 18-19

The Meaning of July Fourth for the Negro 21
- Activating Prior Knowledge 23
- Wrap-up Discussion Questions 32
- Teaching Suggestions 33
- Graphic Organizer A 34

The Gettysburg Address 37
- Activating Prior Knowledge 39
- Wrap-up Discussion Questions 48
- Teaching Suggestions 49
- Graphic Organizer A 50

The New Colossus 53
- Activating Prior Knowledge 55
- Wrap-up Discussion Questions 64
- Teaching Suggestions 65
- Graphic Organizer A 66
- Handout B 67

About the Author 69

Ralph Waldo Emerson's
Self-Reliance

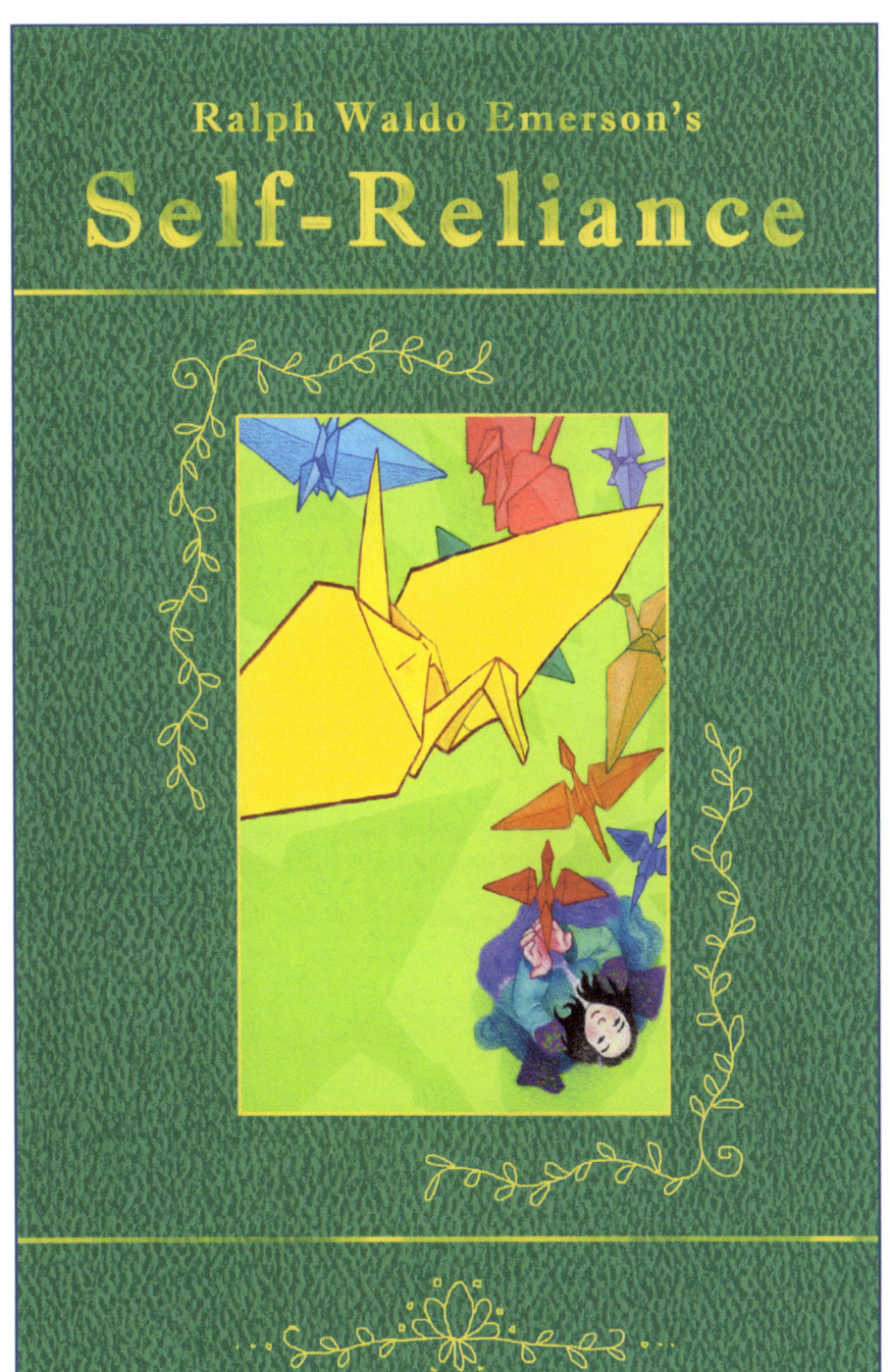

Note to Teacher on Context:

The essay *Self-Reliance* is more than 10,000 words long. These lines are taken from a section near the end in which Emerson expounds on the "rage of travelling" and the misguided desire to follow exotic traditions: *"But the rage of travelling is a symptom of a deeper unsoundness affecting the whole intellectual action. … We imitate; and what is imitation but the travelling of the mind? Our houses are built with foreign taste; our shelves are garnished with foreign ornaments; our opinions, our tastes, our faculties, lean, and follow the Past and the Distant. The soul created the arts wherever they have flourished. It was in his own mind that the artist sought his model. It was an application of his own thought to the thing to be done and the conditions to be observed. And why need we copy the Doric or the Gothic model? Beauty, convenience, grandeur of thought, and quaint expression are as near to us as to any, and if the American artist will study with hope and love the precise thing to be done by him, considering the climate, the soil, the length of the day, the wants of the people, the habit and form of the government, he will create a house in which all these will find themselves fitted, and taste and sentiment will be satisfied also … "*

Notes: _____

_____

_____

_____

_____

_____

Introduction

Ralph Waldo Emerson was a writer, speaker, and philosopher. He also served as a Unitarian minister for several years. Although he was a minister, Emerson began to feel that organized religion was not helpful to people. People needed to trust their own thoughts and feelings, rather than what their church told them. Only then would they find the truth. This belief was called "transcendentalism."

Ralph Waldo Emerson

At the core of transcendentalism was belief in oneself. Emerson thought people should be true to themselves, and have faith in their own minds. They should not just try to do what they have seen others do; nor should they only repeat what they have heard others say.

Emerson explained his philosophy in his essay *Self-Reliance*. It was published in 1841. At the time, Emerson's ideas were very new and even scary to many people. But they caught on. Emerson helped build the idea of American individualism.

What Is a Primary Source?

A primary source is a piece of history. It is an artifact from a time period, like a diary, a speech, a newspaper article, or a photograph. In this chapter, you will study the essay *Self-Reliance* as a primary source from 1841, as a way to learn about that time period of American history.

Activating Prior Knowledge: Questions for Pre-Reading Discussion

1. What kinds of activities are you really good at?
2. How did you discover you had these talents?
3. What do you think is the best way to develop your talents?
4. Have you ever tried a new activity and found you had no interest in it?
5. What do you think of when you hear the phrase "self-reliance"?
6. Who do you "rely" on in your life?
7. What are some ways you rely on yourself?

Vocabulary and Context Questions

Complete this page as you read. Using context clues and/or a dictionary, define each word:

Vocabulary

reliance: *trust or confidence*

insist: *keep fighting for*

imitate: *copy or duplicate*

cultivation: *development*

adopted: *taken on what belongs to someone else*

possession: *ownership*

exhibited: *shown*

unique: *one of a kind*

assigned: *given to*

Context Questions

1. Who wrote this essay? *Ralph Waldo Emerson*

2. When did he write it? *1841*

3. What was his purpose? *To express his philosophy and beliefs*

4. Who read this essay? *American citizens, citizens of other countries where it was printed*

Supplementary Information

- These lines are a core belief of transcendentalism. Other transcendentalists included Henry David Thoreau and Margaret Fuller.

- In 1836, Emerson was a founding member of The Transcendental Club. This was a group of New England intellectuals. Their journal, which they began publishing in the 1840s, was called *The Dial*.

- Other prominent writers of the time, including Nathaniel Hawthorne, were critical of the Transcendentalist Movement.

- In another part of this essay, Emerson echoes these lines with, *"Whoso would be a man must be a non-conformist."*

Comprehension and Discussion Questions

- Emerson says you should "insist on" whom? *Yourself.*

- What do you think he means by that? *Be yourself; be true to what you believe, always stand up for your ideals, even when you are discouraged, you must "insist."*

- What does Emerson say you should "never" do? *Imitate.*

- Do you think this is good advice? Are there times when it is good to imitate? *Answers will vary. Students may say that imitation can be useful when learning how to do something, whether it is learning to tie your shoes, building a model airplane, or using good manners.*

Insist on yourself; never imitate.

Notes: _____

_____

_____

_____

_____

Your own gift you can present every moment with the force of a whole life's cultivation; but of the adopted talent of another, you have only half possession.

Supplementary Information

- Emerson went to the Harvard University Divinity School, studying to become a Unitarian minister — like his father had been.
- He graduated in 1829, and the next year Emerson became Pastor of the Second Unitarian Church of Boston.
- Differences of opinion with the church — Emerson did not want to give communion — led to his resignation in 1832.
- In his writings and speeches, Emerson continued to challenge traditional forms of organized religion. His philosophy of individualism greatly impacted many American churches.

Comprehension and Discussion Questions

- What does Emerson mean by "your own gift"? *Your true talent, those things you are truly good at, your real passion, your "bliss."*
- What does he mean by "the adopted talent of another"? *Something you've seen someone else do, but for which you do not have a natural affinity or gift. Students also may suggest these lines refer to activities or sports their parents or teachers encourage in them, but for which they themselves do not believe they have a natural talent.*
- Have you ever heard the proverb, "Bloom where you're planted"? How does Emerson's essay compare to that proverb? *It is similar. Emerson is saying you will always do better at expressing your "own gift," than you will at trying to do what someone else is good at.*

Notes:

_____
_____
_____
_____
_____
_____
_____
_____
_____

Supplementary Information

- Throughout *Self-Reliance*, Emerson is critical of organized religion, which he believes stifles the creativity of each unique soul. In these lines, Emerson talks of each person being taught as an individual by his Maker. There is no mention of a minister, priest, or church community acting as a mediator.

Comprehension and Discussion Questions

- Who does Emerson say can teach people what they do best? *Only their "Maker" or their God.*

- Do you think Emerson believes people are naturally good, or naturally bad? Explain. *Emerson believes people are naturally good. Further, he believes each of us has within us a secret gift, and no one knows what it is until we show it to the world.*

- Emerson believes all people have a special gift or talent. Do you agree? *Answers will vary.*

Notes: _____
_____
_____
_____
_____
_____
_____
_____
_____
_____

That which each can do best, none but his Maker can teach him. No man yet knows what it is, nor can, till that person has exhibited it.

_____
_____
_____
_____
_____
_____

Where is the master who could have taught Shakespeare? Where is the master who could have instructed Franklin, or Washington, or Bacon, or Newton?

Supplementary Information

- At the time Emerson was writing, America was in the process of defining itself as distinct from Europe. The United States had been independent politically for only three generations. Emerson wanted the country to become independent culturally and intellectually as well as politically.

- Emerson lists both American and European thinkers here, putting the Americans on par with their British counterparts.

- In other writings, Emerson urged Americans that they no longer needed to be influenced by Europeans, and should begin paving their own way.

- Others from this time period shared this sentiment, including Henry Clay, who said, "We look too much abroad. ... Let us become real and true Americans."

- In addition to British playwright William Shakespeare, Emerson refers to American inventor and philosopher Benjamin Franklin, General and first U.S. President George Washington, British philosopher Francis Bacon, and British physicist Isaac Newton.

Comprehension and Discussion Questions

- Why does Emerson name these famous people? *Because they were geniuses in their fields — writing, philosophy, politics, or science. Emerson believes they were not great because they had great teachers, but because they relied on themselves and developed their own talents.*

- Where does Emerson mean to say that these great men's genius comes from? *From something inside themselves, which was taught to them by their Makers.*

- Is Emerson saying these people had no teachers at all? *No, but he is implying that they did not rely on those teachers to direct them; instead they relied on themselves while learning what they could from others.*

Supplementary Information

- Elsewhere in the essay, Emerson states, *"Whoso would be a man must be a non-conformist."* Further, the challenge of self-reliance is living in a society that values tradition and custom, rather than independence and innovation.

- In another section of *Self-Reliance*, Emerson famously states, *"To be great is to be misunderstood."* He lists Pythagoras, Socrates, Jesus Christ, Copernicus and Galileo as men who were misunderstood in their time but whose ideas were proven true by history.

- The benefit of living in a free society is that the true self is allowed to be cultivated.

- Further, Emerson says, *"It is easy in the world to live after the world's opinion; it is easy in solitude to live after our own; but the great man is he who in the midst of the crowd keeps with perfect sweetness the independence of solitude."*

Comprehension and Discussion Questions

- What does "unique" mean? *Exceptional, unlike any other*

- Does Emerson mean that only men can be great? *No. Emerson is using "man" to mean "person." Emerson seemed to view women as intellectually equal to men. He collaborated on a journal with Margaret Fuller and corresponded with several women writers.*

- What "great" people can you think of, from history and in your own life? Are they all unique? In what way? *Answers will vary.*

Every great man is unique.

Notes: _____

Shakespeare will never be made by the study of Shakespeare.

Supplementary Information

- Emerson insists that to be truly great, one can never merely imitate what others have done.

Comprehension and Discussion Questions

- How would you put this phrase in your own words? *Merely studying a great writer will never make you a great writer.*

- Emerson is saying that only studying great writers will never make you a great writer. What else, then, must you do to become a great writer? *Write.*

Notes: _____

_____
_____
_____
_____
_____
_____
_____
_____
_____
_____
_____
_____
_____
_____
_____
_____
_____
_____
_____
_____
_____
_____
_____
_____

Supplementary Information

- The Unitarian Church came to embrace Emerson's beliefs, and claimed transcendentalism as part of its legacy.
- The "sage of Concord," as Emerson was known, died of pneumonia in 1882.

Comprehension and Discussion Questions

- What does Emerson say you should do? *"That which is assigned you."*
- What do you think he means by "that which is assigned you"? *That special gift or talent that your Maker has given you.*
- Are these encouraging words? Explain. *They are encouraging because Emerson is saying that "the sky is the limit" for people pursuing their true talents.*
- What do you think Emerson would say about someone who attempts something and fails over and over? *That person should ask if what they are attempting is their own true gift, or whether it is the gift of another they are trying to imitate. If it is their own true gift, then they should "insist on" themselves and not give up. However, if it is "the adopted talent of another" that they are trying to do — which seems likely if they repeatedly fail — then they should stop imitating and do that which is "assigned" them.*

Notes: _____

_____

_____

_____

Do that which is assigned you, and you cannot hope too much or dare too much.

Self-Reliance

Insist on yourself; never imitate.

Your own gift you can present every moment
with the force of a whole life's cultivation;

but of the adopted talent of another,
you have only half possession.

That which each can do best,
none but his Maker can teach him.

No man yet knows what it is, nor can,
till that person has exhibited it.

Where is the master who could have
taught Shakespeare?

Where is the master who could have instructed
Franklin, or Washington, or Bacon, or Newton?

Every great man is unique.

Shakespeare will never be made
by the study of Shakespeare.

Do that which is assigned you,
and you cannot hope too much or dare too much.

Name: _____ Date: _____

Wrap-up Discussion Questions

- Do you agree with Emerson that everyone has a special gift or talent?

- What do you believe is your special gift?

- How can people figure out what their gift is?

- Which would Emerson think is worse, someone who imitates others, or someone who never tries anything?

- At the time Emerson was writing, the idea of trusting yourself rather than your church was shocking to many people. Do you think it would be as shocking now? Why or why not?

Teaching Suggestions

Activity I: Close Reading

Separate the class into pairs or trios and give each group a slip with an excerpt from *Self-Reliance* (**Graphic Organizer A**). Have them put the sentence(s) in their own words. After a few moments, reconvene the class and distribute complete copies of **Handout A** to each student. Have groups read their paraphrases in turn, and discuss each as a class and decide if it is a faithful and complete paraphrase. Have students complete the chart on **Handout A** with the class paraphrases. When all slips are completed, read the original version of *Self-Reliance* aloud and discuss how the class version compared with the original.

Activity II: Journaling

1. Spend some time in class brainstorming ways students can practice self-reliance. Keep a running list on the board as students share ideas. Then have students keep a "Self-Reliance Journal" for 48 hours. Have them note times and events where they practiced "self-reliance," in other words, when they relied on themselves to be responsible, to act on the desire to try something new, and remained true to themselves when others wanted them to simply conform.

2. Ask students to choose one event from their journal in **Activity II** and write a longer journal-style entry explaining the event and their feelings about it.

Activity III: Synthesis

Have students complete **Handout B: Self-Discovery**. Have them choose one of the statements (1–6) and use it to develop a longer journal-style entry.

Activity IV: Application

1. Cut out and distribute the cards on **Handout C: Self-Reliance Cards**. Depending on the skill level of your students, you could:

- Give individual students all three cards and have them work individually.
- Give one card to each student and have them work individually.
- Separate the class into pairs or trios and have groups complete 1–3 cards.
- Put up an overhead of **Handout C** and go over the scenarios as a class.

2. Once cards 1–3 are completed, have students create their own scenario for the fourth, blank card. They should then trade cards with a partner and complete them. Finally, invite students to share what they wrote, and discuss the student cards as a large group.

Name: _____ Date: _____

Graphic Organizer A

Insist on yourself; never imitate.	*Put this passage in your own words:*
Your own gift you can present every moment with the force of a whole life's cultivation; but of the adopted talent of another, you have only half possession.	*Put this passage in your own words:*
That which each can do best, none but his Maker can teach him. No man yet knows what it is, nor can, till that person has exhibited it.	*Put this passage in your own words:*
Where is the master who could have taught Shakespeare? Where is the master who could have instructed Franklin, or Washington, or Bacon, or Newton?	*Put this passage in your own words:*
Every great man is unique.	*Put this passage in your own words:*
Shakespeare will never be made by the study of Shakespeare.	*Put this passage in your own words:*
Do that which is assigned you, and you cannot hope too much or dare too much.	*Put this passage in your own words:*

Name: _____ Date: _____

Handout B: Self-Discovery

1. I think I am really good at _____

   _____ .

2. I knew I was good at it when _____

   _____ .

3. When I do _____ (No.1–2), I feel _____

   _____ .

4. I've always wanted to try _____

   _____ .

5. When I imagine myself doing _____ (No. 3), I feel _____

   _____ .

6. When I think of myself in ten years, I imagine being self-reliant when I _____

   _____

   _____ .

Name: _____ Date: _____

Handout C: Self-Reliance Cards

Directions: Read cards 1–3 and circle what the self-reliant action would be. Then write a one-sentence explanation. Then write your own card and trade with a partner.

---

1. School is over, and the gym is closed until tomorrow. Some of your friends want to break into the gym and play with the equipment. Everyone seems to be going along with the idea, but you know it is wrong, and you could get in trouble.

    A. Go along with them. You might get in trouble, but it would be fun to play basketball.

    B. Tell them you are not interested in breaking the rules, and suggest a park or other place where you could play without getting into trouble.

    Explanation: _____
    _____

---

2. You love writing poetry, and you believe you are pretty good at it. You even won a "best poem" award last year in school. Your parents, however, want you to stop writing poetry and concentrate on math. You are getting Cs in math, maybe because you are writing poems instead of doing your math homework.

    A. Tell you parents you refuse to try any harder at math because it is clear that since you are getting Cs, you were not meant to be doing it.

    B. Agree to try harder at math, because you haven't really given it your all this year. But find some time to develop your love of poetry as well.

    Explanation: _____
    _____

Name: _____   Date: _____

Handout C: Self-Reliance Cards

3. You love science, and you just won first prize in the school science fair. Your science teacher has offered to help you take your exhibit to the county fair. But your brother keeps telling you to give it up because you will never win.

A. Tell your teacher thanks, but no thanks. You'd never win against all those smart kids at the county fair.

B. Ignore your brother and accept your teacher's offer to go to the county fair. You believe you have a good chance of winning. Even if you don't win, it would be a great experience to go.

Explanation: _____
_____

4. Write your own card here, and then trade it with a partner's card.

Explanation: _____
_____

Frederick Douglass
JULY 4th

What, to the American slave, is your 4th of July?

I answer; a day that reveals to the slave, more than any all other days in the year, the gross injustice and cruelty to which he is the constant victim.

To him, your celebration is a sham: your nat- -ional greatness, swelling vanity; Your sounds of rejoicing are empty and heart- -less; your shout of liberty and equality, hollow  mockery;

Your prayers and hymns, your sermons and thanks- givings are to the slave, fraud and hypocrisy.

A thin veil to cover up crimes which would disgrace a nation of savages.

There is not a nation on the earth guilty of prac- -tices more shocking and bloody than are the people of the United States at this

Note to Teacher on Context:

Douglass began his speech by expressing his great admiration for the work and deeds of the Founding Fathers, but he quickly added that his view of them was "not the most favorable." What, he asked, had the Declaration of Independence meant for black people? He asked rhetorically, "Would you have me argue that man is entitled to liberty? That he is the rightful owner of his own body? You have already declared it."

Notes: _____

_____
_____
_____
_____
_____
_____
_____
_____
_____
_____
_____
_____
_____
_____
_____
_____
_____

Introduction

Frederick Douglass was born a slave in Maryland. He escaped in 1838, and traveled to freedom in New York. He soon joined with other people who were working to end slavery in the United States. Fighting for equality became his life's work.

Frederick Douglass

When he was 23, Douglass gave his first speech. He was a great speaker and impressed many in the audience. He was soon asked to give a series of lectures on slavery. Douglass wrote a book, published a newspaper, and continued speaking out about why slavery was wrong.

On July 5, 1852, Douglass spoke to a crowd in Rochester, New York. It was the day after Independence Day. Douglass believed that it was not right for Americans to celebrate their freedom when American slaves had no freedom. He decided to make his speech about what the Fourth of July meant to a slave. He hoped to encourage more Americans to work to end slavery.

Douglass lived to see slavery banned in the United States in 1865. He had worked his entire life for that goal and for the equality of all people.

What Is a Primary Source?

A primary source is a piece of history. It is an artifact from a time period, like a diary, a speech, a newspaper article, or a photograph. In this chapter, you will study the speech *The Meaning of July Fourth for the Negro* as a primary source from 1852, as a way to learn about that time period of American history.

_____
_____
_____
_____
_____
_____

Activating Prior Knowledge: Questions for Pre-Reading Discussion

1. Why do Americans celebrate the Fourth of July?
2. What do you think are the best things about that holiday?
3. Have you heard of Frederick Douglass? What do you know about him?
4. What do you know about the history of slavery in the United States?
5. How do you think slaves felt when whites celebrated the Fourth of July?

Vocabulary and Context Questions

Complete this page as you read. Using context clues and/or a dictionary, define each word:

Vocabulary

gross: *very large*

injustice: *unfairness*

sham: *fake*

liberty: *freedom*

hollow: *empty*

mockery: *making a joke of something*

fraud: *phony*

hypocrisy: *saying one thing and doing another, being two-faced*

despair: *lose hope for*

doom: *the end of*

Context Questions

1. Who wrote this speech? *Frederick Douglass*

2. When did he write it? *1852*

3. What was his purpose? *To open people's eyes to why slavery was wrong, and to argue that Americans were being hypocritical (two-faced) in celebrating "freedom" on the Fourth of July.*

4. Who heard or read this speech? *The audience at the Rochester, New York, speech, but also Americans across the country — both North and South.*

Supplementary Information

- This question sets the stage for the rest of his speech. Frederick Douglass will argue that Independence Day celebrations are hypocritical in a country that tolerates slavery.

- Douglass was giving this speech in New York, which was a free state.

- The people in his audience were already convinced that slavery was wrong, but some may have believed they did not have a responsibility to end slavery in other states.

- Douglass wanted Northerners to believe that it was not enough to ban slavery in their own states — allowing it to continue in the South was morally wrong.

- Douglass knew his speech would be reprinted throughout the country.

Comprehension and Discussion Questions

- How would you re-state Douglass' question? *What does the Fourth of July mean to an enslaved person in America?*

- Do you think this was a question many people asked? *Answers will vary.*

- How do you think Douglass will go on to answer that question? *Answers will vary.*

- How do you think the audience felt to hear him say *"your 4th of July?" The word "your" reminded the audience that they, personally and individually, had some responsibility in what Douglass was about to discuss.*

What, to the American slave, is your Fourth of July?

18

Notes: _____
_____
_____
_____
_____
_____

I answer; a day that reveals to the slave, more than all other days in the year, the gross injustice and cruelty to which he is the constant victim.

Comprehension and Discussion Questions

- What does Douglass say happens on the Fourth of July? *More than any other day of the year, enslaved people understood how unfair their treatment was.*

- What is the "gross injustice" Douglass is talking about? *Slavery*

- Why would the Fourth of July be a special reminder of the injustice of slavery? *Because it is a day when Americans celebrate their freedom — but slaves have no freedom. They are denied their freedom in a society that practices and tolerates slavery.*

Notes:

_____
_____
_____
_____
_____
_____
_____
_____
_____
_____
_____
_____
_____
_____
_____
_____
_____
_____

Supplementary Information

- In another section of the speech, Douglass ironically points out Americans' "denunciation of tyrants." He believes it is ironic for Americans to condemn the tyranny of the British king, when so many of them are tyrants themselves by "owning" human beings.

- Founding Father (and slave-owner) George Mason expressed a similar idea, saying "Every master is born a petty tyrant."

Supplementary Information

- Douglass deliberately chose his words and phrases to arouse the emotions of his listeners. He believed the situation called for it. In another section of the speech, he explains: "At a time like this, scorching irony, not convincing argument, is needed. O! had I the ability, and could reach the nation's ear, I would, to-day, pour out a fiery stream of biting ridicule, blasting reproach, withering sarcasm, and stern rebuke. For it is not light that is needed, but fire; it is not the gentle shower, but thunder. We need the storm, the whirlwind, and the earthquake. The feeling of the nation must be quickened; the conscience of the nation must be roused …"

Comprehension and Discussion Questions

- What does Douglass mean by "a sham"? *It is a fake. It cannot be real. Americans cannot truly be celebrating freedom when they themselves deny freedom to an entire race of people.*

- How do you think white Americans felt hearing these words? *Answers will vary. Students may say they felt angry, guilty, indignant, ashamed, and perhaps motivated to work for change.*

Notes: _____
_____
_____
_____
_____
_____

To him, your celebration is a sham; your national greatness, swelling vanity.

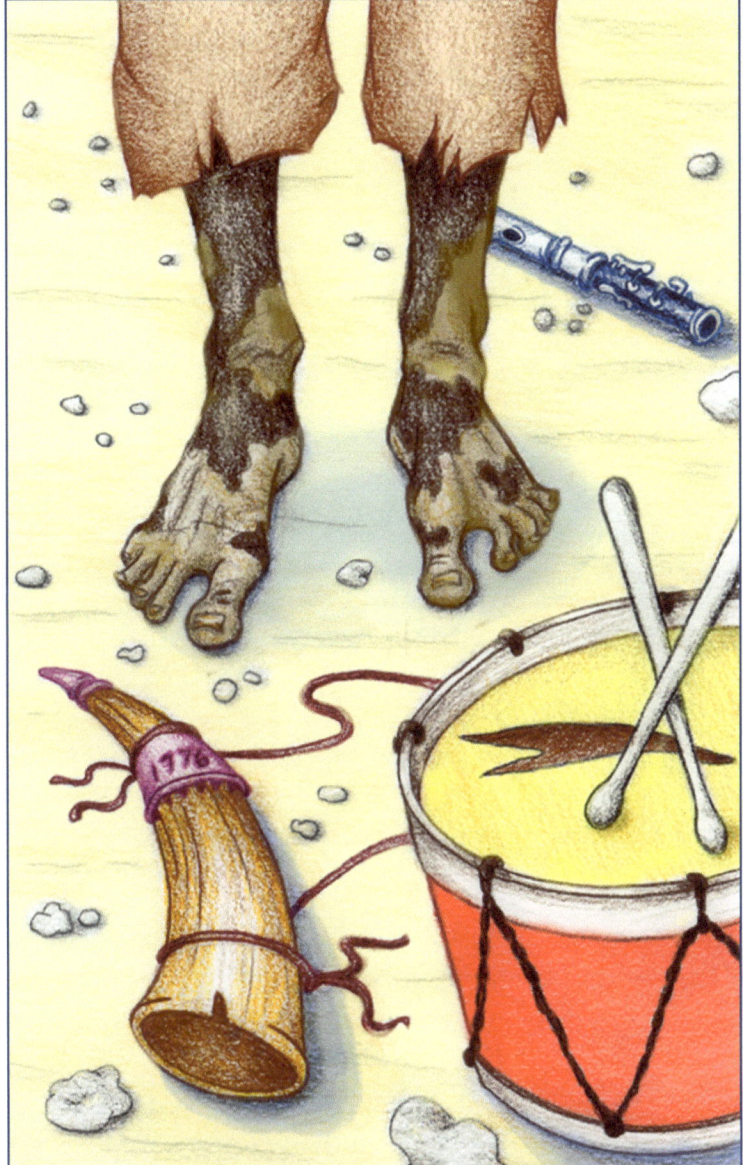

Your sounds of rejoicing are empty and heartless; your shout of liberty and equality, hollow mockery.

Comprehension and Discussion Questions

- What sounds of rejoicing might Douglass mean? *Music, fireworks, drums, singing, people's laughter and happy voices*
- Why does he call these sounds "heartless"? *They are made while ignoring the reality of slavery. They are not sounds of true joy; they are phony.*
- What does Douglass say about Americans' "shout of liberty and equality"? *They are false. They don't mean anything. Americans say they love liberty and equality, but they really don't because they deny slaves their freedom.*
- Do you agree with what Douglass is saying? Is he right about 1852 America? *Answers will vary.*

Notes:
_____
_____
_____
_____
_____
_____
_____
_____
_____
_____
_____
_____
_____
_____
_____
_____

Supplementary Information

- Douglass uses terms from the Declaration of Independence to cast doubt on Americans' sincere belief in them. The Declaration states, "all men are created *equal*" with inalienable rights including *"liberty."*
- Douglass accuses Americans of a "shout of liberty." In the past, some British observers made similar comments. British author Samuel Johnson asked how it was "that we hear the loudest yelps for liberty among the drivers of Negroes."

Supplementary Information

- This sentiment was shared by many of the Founding Fathers. For example, John Jay wrote in 1786, "It is much to be wished that slavery may be abolished. To contend for our own liberty, and to deny that blessing to others, involves an inconsistency not to be excused."

- While some Christians were abolitionists, many others used the Bible to justify slavery. Douglass found this particularly wrong. "What, then, remains to be argued? Is it that slavery is not divine; that God did not establish it; that our doctors of divinity are mistaken? That which is inhuman, cannot be divine!"

- In another section, Douglass says slavery is a crime against God and man: "the hypocrisy of the nation must be exposed; and its crimes against God and man must be proclaimed and denounced."

- Many white Americans believed their culture was more civilized than that of American Indians, who they sometimes called "savages." The phrase "a nation of savages" called attention to the reality that there was nothing civilized about slavery. Those who owned slaves or condoned slavery were worse than savages.

Comprehension and Discussion Questions

- What does Douglass say is a fraud in these lines? *Americans' religious expressions.*

- Why does Douglass say Americans pray and give thanks

Your prayers and hymns, your sermons and thanksgivings are to the slave, fraud and hypocrisy. A thin veil to cover up crimes which would disgrace a nation of savages.

to God? *To cover up their crimes against God and man in the practice of slavery. To seem like good people, while in reality they are criminals.*

- What does he mean when he says America's crimes would "disgrace a nation of savages"? *Americans think they are civilized, but really they are worse than savages.*

There is not a nation on the earth guilty of practices more shocking and bloody than are the people of the United States, at this very hour.

Comprehension and Discussion Questions

- Why do you think Douglass adds, "at this very hour"? *As a reminder that slavery is ongoing. It adds urgency to what he is saying.*

- What do you think Douglass wanted his audience to feel when they heard these words? *Shame, guilt, sadness, a desire to change.*

Notes: _____

Supplementary Information

- Douglass continued in his speech: "Go where you may, search where you will, roam through all the monarchies and despotisms of the Old World, travel through South America, search out every abuse, and when you have found the last, lay your facts by the side of the everyday practices of this nation, and you will say with me, that, for revolting barbarity and shameless hypocrisy, America reigns without a rival. ..."

Supplementary Information

- These lines mark a dramatic shift in the tone of Douglass' speech. He has been painting a very bleak picture of the country, but now says he is hopeful.

- Douglass explains that he draws encouragement from the principles of the Declaration of Independence and the "genius" of American institutions.

- Douglass also finds hope in the "tendencies of the age." He says, "No nation can now shut itself up from the surrounding world. ... Walled cities and empires have become unfashionable. ... Oceans no longer divide, but link nations together."

- This speech was given nine years before the start of the Civil War. Thirteen years later in 1865, the Thirteenth Amendment was ratified, ending slavery in the United States.

- Douglass was an adviser to President Abraham Lincoln and later held positions during the Reconstruction Era.

Comprehension and Discussion Questions

- Why does Douglass still have hope for the United States? *Because of movements within the country that are working to end slavery, and because of God's grace.*

- What do you think are some of those "forces" Douglass is thinking of? *The Abolitionist Movement in America. People are speaking and writing about the evils of slavery. People were writing letters to Congress [called*

[But] I do not despair of this country. There are forces which must work the downfall of slavery. "The arm of the Lord is not shortened," and the doom of slavery is certain.

24

petitions], and raising awareness of the issue. Douglass may also have meant divine forces, meaning God was working in the hearts and minds of citizens. Some of his listeners may have beliefs that they themselves were those "forces" Douglass mentioned.

- How do you feel after reading Douglass' speech? *Answers will vary.*

The Meaning of July Fourth for the Negro

What, to the American slave, is your Fourth of July?

I answer; a day that reveals to the slave,
more than all other days in the year,
the gross injustice and cruelty to which
he is the constant victim.

To him, your celebration is a sham;
your national greatness, swelling vanity.
Your sounds of rejoicing are empty and heartless;
your shout of liberty and equality, hollow mockery.

Your prayers and hymns,
your sermons and thanks-givings
are to the slave, fraud and hypocrisy.

A thin veil to cover up crimes
which would disgrace a nation of savages.
There is not a nation on the earth guilty of practices
more shocking and bloody than are the people of
the United States, at this very hour.

[But] I do not despair of this country. There are
forces which must work the downfall of slavery.

"The arm of the Lord is not shortened,"
and the doom of slavery is certain.

Name: _____ Date: _____

Wrap-up Discussion Questions

- How do you think people felt listening to Frederick Douglass' speech?

- What kind of person does Douglass seem to be?

- Why do you think Frederick Douglass used words from the Declaration of Independence in his speech?

- Why do you think he chose to speak about what the Fourth of July meant to an American slave? Why did he choose that holiday?

- How do you think Douglass felt when the Thirteenth Amendment to the Constitution was passed in 1865, ending slavery in the United States?

Teaching Suggestions

Activity I: Close Reading

Separate the class into pairs or trios and give each group a slip of paper with an excerpt from *The Meaning of July Fourth for the Negro* (**Graphic Organizer A**). Have them put the sentence(s) in their own words. After a few moments, reconvene the class and distribute complete copies of **Handout A** to each student. Have groups read their paraphrases in turn, and discuss each as a class and decide if it is a faithful and complete paraphrase. Have students complete the chart on **Handout A** with the class paraphrases. When all slips are completed, read the original version of *The Meaning of July Fourth for the Negro* aloud, and discuss how the class version compared with the original.

Activity II: Compare and Contrast

Give students library and/or computer time to research what Fourth of July celebrations were like in the 19th century. They should learn the answers to these and other questions:

- Did fireworks exist in the 1800s?
- What songs did people sing to celebrate the Fourth of July?
- What foods were common at celebrations?
- What was the Fourth of July like for a slave?
- Did slaves celebrate the holiday?
- How does all of this information compare with modern Fourth of July celebrations?

Activity III: Creative Writing

Ask students to imagine that they will be going to see Frederick Douglass give a speech, and that after the speech he will have a question-and-answer period. Have them prepare three questions they might ask Douglass if given the chance. Allow students some time to research the answers to the questions, and share what they learned with the class.

Name: _____   Date: _____

Graphic Organizer A

What, to the American slave, is your Fourth of July?	*Put this passage in your own words:*
I answer; a day that reveals to the slave, more than all other days in the year, the gross injustice and cruelty to which he is the constant victim.	*Put this passage in your own words:*
To him, your celebration is a sham; your national greatness, swelling vanity.	*Put this passage in your own words:*
Your sounds of rejoicing are empty and heartless; your shout of liberty and equality, hollow mockery.	*Put this passage in your own words:*
Your prayers and hymns, your sermons and thanks-givings are to the slave, fraud and hypocrisy. A thin veil to cover up crimes which would disgrace a nation of savages.	*Put this passage in your own words:*
There is not a nation on the earth guilty of practices more shocking and bloody than are the people of the United States, at this very hour.	*Put this passage in your own words:*
[But] I do not despair of this country. There are forces which must work the downfall of slavery. "The arm of the Lord is not shortened," and the doom of slavery is certain.	*Put this passage in your own words:*

The Gettysburg Address

Four score and seven years ago our fathers brought forth, on this continent, a new nation...

Note to Teacher on Context:

The *Gettysburg Address* is reproduced here almost in its entirety. One significant passage following "that the nation might live ..." has been deleted for reasons of length and vocabulary. *"But, in a larger sense, we cannot dedicate — we cannot consecrate — we cannot hallow — this ground. The brave men, living and dead, who struggled here, have consecrated it, far above our poor power to add or detract."*

Notes: _____

_____
_____
_____
_____
_____
_____
_____
_____
_____
_____
_____
_____
_____
_____
_____

Introduction

Abraham Lincoln

One of the bloodiest battles of the Civil War was the Battle of Gettysburg. An estimated 8,000 men were killed during that three-day battle, which took place in July 1863. Altogether there were about 51,000 total casualties that included soldiers killed, wounded, captured or missing. When the Union troops won, the battle was over, but the war went on.

It was time to bury the dead, and plans were made for a National Cemetery. President Abraham Lincoln was invited to Gettysburg, Pennsylvania, to give a speech at the dedication of the cemetery. President Lincoln wanted to honor the Union soldiers who had fought and died at Gettysburg. But he also had another purpose. He wanted to give new meaning to the soldiers' sacrifice.

Until then, Lincoln had always said the purpose of the Civil War was to save the Union. While giving the speech — called the *Gettysburg Address* — on November 19, 1863, Lincoln said the purpose of the Civil War was to end slavery in the United States. Of even greater importance, Lincoln explained that if the United States was going to live up to its ideals, slavery would have to end.

What Is a Primary Source?

A primary source is a piece of history. It is an artifact from a time period, like a diary, a speech, a newspaper article, or a photograph. In this chapter, you will study the speech the *Gettysburg Address* as a primary source from 1863, as a way to learn about that time period of American history.

28

_____
_____
_____
_____
_____

Activating Prior Knowledge: Questions for Pre-Reading Discussion

1. What do you know about the Civil War?
2. What do you know about Abraham Lincoln? Can you list some of his most important achievements as President of the United States?
3. What do you know about the history of slavery in the United States?
4. Have you ever heard the phrase "actions speak louder than words"? What does it mean? Do you agree?
5. Abraham Lincoln wanted to encourage Americans to live up to the country's ideals. What are some of those?
6. How do you live up to American ideals in your own life?

Vocabulary and Context Questions

Complete this page as you read. Using context clues and/or a dictionary, define each word:

Vocabulary

score: *twenty years*

conceived: *created*

liberty: *freedom*

dedicated: *devoted or committed to*

proposition: *idea*

endure: *go on*

advanced: *worked for*

resolve: *promise*

in vain: *for nothing*

perish: *die away*

Context Questions

1. Who wrote this speech? *President Abraham Lincoln*

2. When did he write it? *1863*

3. What was his purpose? *To dedicate a cemetery for Union soldiers at the Battle of Gettysburg*

4. Who heard or read the *Gettysburg Address*? *The audience members at the dedication of the military cemetery; Americans across the country — both North and South*

Supplementary Information

- The text of the *Gettysburg Address* is carved into the south wall of the Lincoln Memorial in Washington, D.C.
- There are no photographs of Lincoln delivering his speech. One reason for this may be that photographers in the 19th century needed a great deal of time to ready their equipment, and they did not realize Lincoln's speech was going to be so short.
- About 15,000 people attended the dedication of the National Cemetery.
- Lincoln uses a series of metaphors in the *Gettysburg Address* that compare the history of the United States to the birth and development of a human life. The first of these appears in these lines: "our fathers brought forth."

Comprehension and Discussion Questions

- Four score and seven years ago means 87 years ago. Lincoln was speaking in 1863. What event is he referring to? *The issuing of the Declaration of Independence in 1776, proclaiming the United States as a new nation separate from England.*
- Why does Lincoln say "our fathers"? *He is referring to his and his audiences' ancestors — whether by blood or by belief in the ideals of the new nation.*

Notes: _____
_____
_____
_____

Four score and seven years ago our fathers brought forth on this continent a new nation,

_____
_____
_____
_____

conceived in Liberty, and dedicated to the proposition that all men are created equal.

Supplementary Information

- Lincoln continues the metaphor of the United States as a living being with the word "conceived."
- The words "all men are created equal" are taken from the Declaration of Independence, written by Thomas Jefferson in 1776.
- As the Founding Fathers understood these words, all people, regardless of their birthplace, were created with an equality of rights.

Among these, the Declaration continues, are "life, liberty, and the pursuit of happiness."

- Slavery was an important topic at the Constitutional Convention. Many wished for it to be banned in all the states, but feared union would be impossible if this demand was made. Gouverneur Morris of Pennsylvania called slavery a "nefarious institution, the curse of heaven on the states where it prevails."

Comprehension and Discussion Questions

- What do you think Lincoln means by "conceived in Liberty"? *The idea for America came out of liberty. The idea for America was created by people who wanted to be free from tyranny of the British king. American ideals of freedom go back to America's founding, and liberty is its most important, essential ideal.*

- Have you heard the phrase "all men are created equal" before? *Answers will vary. Some students will recognize the words from the Declaration of Independence.*

- Why does Lincoln say the United States is "dedicated" to the idea that all men are created equal? *The United States was founded on the ideal of equality. No person was born with the right to rule over others without their consent. This was different from the British system of monarchy, where a king ruled by birth, not through the peoples' consent.*

- Can people be "equal" when slavery is permitted? *Slavery is completely at odds with the idea that all people have equal rights. An enslaved person has no liberty.*

Supplementary Information

- At the time of the *Gettysburg Address*, the Civil War was more than two years old.
- In December 1860, after Lincoln was elected president, South Carolina's legislature voted to secede from the Union. Soon, seven more states seceded. Eventually, eleven states made up the Confederacy.
- In his March 1861 Inaugural Address, Lincoln said he had no plans to interfere with slavery where it already existed.
- Lincoln also said he believed secession was improper and unconstitutional, and he would not accept it.
- The Civil War began in April 1861.
- Lincoln stated consistently in his speeches and writings that his goal in fighting the Civil War was to preserve the Union.
- These lines mark the first time Lincoln states that the Civil War is about the nation's ideal of equality.

Comprehension and Discussion Questions

- What does Lincoln mean by "so conceived and so dedicated"? *Conceived in liberty, and dedicated to the idea that all men are created equal.*
- What does Lincoln say that the Civil War is "testing"? *Whether a country dedicated to liberty and equality will be able to survive. In other words, the citizens of the United States are being tested to see if they are strong enough to fight for their ideals of liberty and equality.*

Now we are engaged in a great civil war, testing whether that nation, or any nation, so conceived and so dedicated, can long endure.

32

Notes:

_____
_____
_____
_____
_____

We are met on a great battle-field of that war. We have come to dedicate a portion of that field, as a final resting place for those who here gave their lives that that nation might live.

Supplementary Information

- Lincoln refers to the Gettysburg Battlefield, and the dedication of the National Cemetery.
- An estimated 8,000 soldiers died during the three-day Battle of Gettysburg.
- The Union soldiers were victorious in this battle, and it is now looked upon as a turning point in the Civil War.

- Lincoln continues his metaphor of the United States as a living being with the words "that that nation might live."

Comprehension and Discussion Questions

- On what battlefield does Lincoln say he and his audience are meeting? *Gettysburg, Pennsylvania.*
- Lincoln says that a portion of the field will be dedicated to the fallen. What does he mean by this? *A military cemetery will be on part of the battlefield.*
- Who are "those who gave their lives"? *The Union soldiers.*
- Why does Lincoln say those soldiers gave their lives? *So that the nation might live.*
- How do you think Lincoln feels about the soldiers' sacrifice? *He feels humbled, grateful, and inspired.*

Notes: _____

_____
_____
_____
_____
_____
_____
_____
_____
_____
_____
_____
_____
_____

Supplementary Information

- The main speaker at the dedication ceremony was famous orator and statesman Edward Everett. In contrast to Lincoln's very brief, ten-sentence speech, Everett spoke for two hours. His speech has been largely forgotten by history, proving Lincoln somewhat correct in these lines.
- More than a century later, Lincoln's *Gettysburg Address* has been long remembered and cherished as an expression of American ideals.

Comprehension and Discussion Questions

- What is the "unfinished work" that Lincoln refers to? *Fighting to save the Union, and ridding the country of slavery.*
- How does Lincoln contrast "what we say here" with "what they [the soldiers] did here"? *The world will soon forget his words, but it will always remember the bravery and sacrifice of the soldiers.*
- Which does Lincoln believe matters more — words, or action? *Answers will vary, but most students will say he believed actions matter more. Lincoln says the world will not remember what he and his fellow speakers say, but it will always remember the soldiers' bravery.*
- What words would you use to describe Lincoln's feelings here? *Modest, humble, respectful.*
- Who does Lincoln say now has the responsibility for helping the United States live up to its ideals? *The living. In other words, all citizens.*

The world will little note, nor long remember what we say here, but it can never forget what they did here. It is for us the living, rather, to be dedicated here to the unfinished work which they who fought here have advanced.

Notes: _____

_____

_____

_____

_____

_____

We here highly resolve that these dead shall not have died in vain — that this nation, under God, shall have a new birth of freedom,

Comprehension and Discussion Questions

- What does Lincoln say he resolves to do? *Make sure the soldiers have not died in vain — in other words, make sure they did not die for nothing.*

- What does Lincoln want for the United States? *A new birth of freedom.*

- What does Lincoln mean by "a new birth of freedom"? *An end to the institution of slavery. The nation will have a new birth of freedom because the population of enslaved persons will be free. In another sense, the national conscience also will be "reborn" with the new understanding that slavery is wrong.*

Notes: _____

_____
_____
_____
_____
_____
_____
_____
_____
_____
_____
_____
_____
_____
_____
_____
_____
_____
_____

Supplementary Information

- Three early drafts of the *Gettysburg Address* written by Lincoln do not contain the words "under God." The later drafts include the phrase.

- Lincoln continues his metaphor of the United States as a living being with the phrase "birth of freedom."

Supplementary Information

- When Lincoln concluded his speech with these lines, there was a hush in the crowd. Accounts differ on whether there was applause, and if so, how much applause there was.
- Some people in the crowd may not have realized President Lincoln had concluded his speech, as his remarks had been so brief.

Comprehension and Discussion Questions

- How does Lincoln describe American government? *Of the people, by the people, for the people. In other words, government is through the consent of the governed.*
- What does Lincoln mean by "perish from the earth"? *Disappear or cease to exist anywhere on Earth.*
- In Abraham Lincoln's view, what will happen if the South wins the Civil War? *The ideals of government the Founding Fathers created will disappear, and the injustice of slavery will continue. No government that is of, by, and for the people can permit slavery. A master rules over a slave without the slave's consent. Slavery denies the natural rights of enslaved persons.*
- Several of the Founders owned slaves. Does this take away from the ideals expressed in the Declaration of Independence? *Answers will vary. Some will say yes, that it shows an unacceptable hypocrisy. Others will say no, that the ideals expressed in the Declaration were ideals even at the time — in other words, something the*

and that government of the people, by the people, for the people, shall not perish from the earth.

Founders were working to achieve even though they did not end slavery everywhere in America during their lifetimes.

Notes: _____

_____

_____

_____

The Gettysburg Address

Four score and seven years ago
our fathers brought forth
on this continent a new nation,
conceived in Liberty, and dedicated
to the proposition that all men are created equal.

Now we are engaged in a great civil war,
testing whether that nation, or any nation,
so conceived and so dedicated, can long endure.

We are met on a great battle-field of that war.
We have come to dedicate a portion of that field,
as a final resting place for those
who here gave their lives that that nation might live.

The world will little note, nor long remember
what we say here,
but it can never forget what they did here.

It is for us the living, rather,
to be dedicated here to the unfinished work
which they who fought here have advanced.

We here highly resolve that these dead shall not
have died in vain — that this nation, under God, shall
have a new birth of freedom,

and that government of the people, by the people,
for the people, shall not perish from the earth.

Name: _____   Date: _____

Wrap-up Discussion Questions

- How do you think people felt listening to President Abraham Lincoln's speech?

- What are the American ideals he describes?

- Do you agree that these are some ideals of America?

- Why do you think President Lincoln used words from the Declaration of Independence in his speech?

- All the states north of Maryland had abolished slavery by 1804. This was fifteen years after the Constitution was ratified. Why do you think the Northern states did not force the Southern states to abolish slavery?

- Why do you think all states did not abolish slavery by themselves?

- President Lincoln's speech is just 293 words. Famous statesman Edward Everett, who was at the cemetery dedication along with Lincoln, spoke for more than two hours. Why do you think history has remembered Lincoln's speech but largely forgotten Everett's?

Teaching Suggestions

Activity I: Close Reading

Separate the class into pairs or trios and give each group a slip of paper with an excerpt from the *Gettysburg Address* (**Graphic Organizer A**). Have them put the sentence(s) in their own words. After a few moments, reconvene the class and distribute complete copies of **Handout A** to each student. Have groups read their paraphrases in turn, and discuss each as a class and decide if it is a faithful and complete paraphrase. Have students complete the chart on **Handout A** with the class paraphrases. When all slips are completed, read the original version of the *Gettysburg Address* aloud and discuss how the class version compared with the original.

Activity II: Compare and Contrast

1. Have students compare the *Gettysburg Address* with other Lincoln statements on the meaning of the Civil War. Write the following sentences on the board or overhead, and read each aloud, making sure students understand them.

   First Inaugural (1861): *"I have no purpose ... to interfere with the institution of slavery in the States where it exists."*

   Letter to Horace Greeley (1862): *"My ... object in this struggle is to save the Union, and is not either to save or to destroy slavery."*

2. As a large class, discuss the following questions:
   - How did Lincoln's stated reasons for the Civil War change over time?
   - Why do you think his reasons changed?
   - Which sounds like the best reason to you?
   - Was Lincoln right to fight the Civil War?

Activity III: Creative Writing

1. Ask students to imagine that they are trying to convince their friends about something that is important to them in their daily lives at school or at home. Have them work in groups to brainstorm initial ideas for topics. Then have them write a short speech of ten sentences — the length of the *Gettysburg Address*.

2. Ask students to write a one-paragraph personal journal entry in response to Lincoln's address. Then, as a class, imagine it is 1864 and discuss how each of the following people might have responded to the speech:
   - A Union soldier
   - A young New Yorker whose older brother is fighting in the Civil War
   - The parent of a fallen Union soldier

Activity IV: Application

Separate the class into three groups. Assign each group either "of the people," "by the people," or "for the people." Allowing time to gather materials, have each group create a poster board collage of images, words, photographs, newspaper clippings, etc., demonstrating how the phrase has applied in history. Display the collages together as a mural and give the students time to view all of them.

Name: _____ Date: _____

Graphic Organizer A

Four score and seven years ago our fathers brought forth on this continent a new nation,	*Put this passage in your own words:*
conceived in Liberty, and dedicated to the proposition that all men are created equal.	*Put this passage in your own words:*
Now we are engaged in a great civil war, testing whether that nation, or any nation, so conceived and so dedicated, can long endure.	*Put this passage in your own words:*
We are met on a great battle-field of that war. We have come to dedicate a portion of that field, as a final resting place for those who here gave their lives that that nation might live.	*Put this passage in your own words:*
The world will little note, nor long remember what we say here, but it can never forget what they did here. It is for us the living, rather, to be dedicated here to the unfinished work which they who fought here have advanced.	*Put this passage in your own words:*
We here highly resolve that these dead shall not have died in vain — that this nation, under God, shall have a new birth of freedom,	*Put this passage in your own words:*
and that government of the people, by the people, for the people, shall not perish from the earth.	*Put this passage in your own words:*

Note to Teacher on Context:

The New Colossus is reproduced here in its entirety.

Notes: _____

Introduction

In 1883, a New York City poet named Emma Lazarus was asked to write a poem for a new statue that France was going to give to the United States. It was going to be called the Statue of Liberty, and it would be placed in New York Harbor. Lazarus wrote a poem called *The New Colossus*, and donated it to help raise money for the statue's pedestal.

Emma Lazarus

In the 1800s, people continued to come to the United States as they had since the early 1600s. These waves of immigrants included European Jews, Irish Catholics, Italians, Poles, Germans, and members of many other groups. They made up the "melting pot" of America. These immigrants often came to America through New York Harbor. When they arrived, the first glimpse of America they saw was often the Statue of Liberty.

Lazarus' poem helped define Lady Liberty. The poem even changed the way people thought of liberty itself. Liberty was not something that Americans got once and for all in 1776. Liberty was something people all over the world were seeking. They came to America to find it. The Statue of Liberty has welcomed immigrants to the United States for more than one hundred years.

What Is a Primary Source?

A primary source is a piece of history. It is an artifact from a time period, like a diary, a speech, a newspaper article, or a photograph. In this chapter, you will study the poem *The New Colossus* as a primary source from 1883, as a way to learn about that time period of American history.

Activating Prior Knowledge: Questions for Pre-Reading Discussion

1. Have you ever seen the Statue of Liberty? In photographs? Or in person?
2. When did your family come to the United States?
3. Did you know the Statue of Liberty has a poem on the pedestal?
4. If you had to guess, what do you think that poem might be about?
5. How do you think immigrants felt (and feel) when they arrived in New York Harbor and saw the Statue of Liberty?
6. Have you ever heard the United States' motto, *"e Pluribus Unum"*? What does it mean?

Vocabulary and Context Questions

Complete this page as you read. Using context clues and/or a dictionary, define each word:

Vocabulary

colossus: *a large statue*

brazen: *too bold*

conquering: *defeating*

mighty: *great and strong*

imprisoned: *captured*

exiles: *people with no homeland*

beacon: *shining light*

storied pomp: *stories of greatness*

yearning: *desiring, wanting*

wretched: *pitiful, miserable*

tempest: *storm*

Context Questions

1. Who wrote this poem? *Emma Lazarus*

2. When did she write it? *1883*

3. What was her purpose? *To raise money for the Statue of Liberty's pedestal, and to give meaning to the statue itself*

4. Who heard or read this poem? *New Yorkers in 1883; today, all visitors to the Statue of Liberty can read it*

Supplementary Information

- The Statue of Liberty was dedicated in 1886. It was not designed to be a symbol of immigration. The statue's placement in New York Harbor, however, meant that immigrant ships bound for Ellis Island sailed past it. It was often the first glimpse of America that immigrants had. It soon became a symbol of the hope and promise of an immigrant America.

- The Statue of Liberty's full name is "Liberty Enlightening the World."

- The statue was a gift to the United States from France to commemorate the United States' centennial.

- *The New Colossus* was written in 1883 but not added to the pedestal of the statue until 1903.

- The "brazen giant of Greek fame" refers to the Colossus of Rhodes, one of the Seven Wonders of the Ancient World. The Colossus was a statue of the Greek God Helios erected on the Greek island of Rhodes. The statue was 100 feet tall and is believed to have stood astride the harbor mouth.

Comprehension and Discussion Questions

- What are some ways the Statue of Liberty differs from the famous Greek statue? *Lady Liberty is not brazen, not conquering, and does not straddle land.*

- Lazarus begins her poem by telling us what the Statue of Liberty is not like. Why do you think she does this? *Answers will vary.*

Notes:

Not like the brazen giant of Greek fame,
With conquering limbs astride from land to land;

Here at our sea-washed, sunset gates shall stand
A mighty woman

43

Supplementary Information

- Lazarus may refer to the ancient statue not only for contrast as in the previous lines, but also because of the Statue of Liberty's classical dress, appearance, and symbolism. Libertas was the ancient Roman goddess of freedom from oppression.
- The Founding Fathers were very interested in the rise and fall of the ancient republics in Greece and Rome.

Comprehension and Discussion Questions

- How does Lazarus describe New York Harbor? *Sea-washed, sunset gates.*
- What form does Lazarus say the Statue of Liberty will take? *A mighty woman.*

Notes: _____

_____
_____
_____
_____
_____
_____
_____
_____
_____
_____
_____
_____
_____
_____
_____
_____
_____
_____
_____
_____
_____
_____
_____
_____

Supplementary Information

- America has always been a nation of immigrants. The earliest settlers came from England to Jamestown in the early 1600s. Even many of the people who wrote the Constitution in 1787 were born in other countries — from Scotland to the West Indies.

- Ellis Island opened in 1892. From then until the federal government imposed restrictions on immigration in 1924, about 16 million immigrants were "processed" at Ellis Island.

Comprehension and Discussion Questions

- What does Lazarus say the Statue of Liberty's torch contains? *Imprisoned lightning.*

- What do you think that might mean? *The torch has captured that energy, that electricity, and will light the world with it. It may be a reference to Benjamin Franklin's experiments with electricity and his invention of the lightning rod.*

- An exile is someone without a home country. How is the Statue of Liberty the "Mother of Exiles"? *She welcomes people who are seeking a new home. She takes care of them and gives them a home. She is welcoming and nurturing. She loves them, and helps them like a mother helps her children.*

Notes: _____
_____
_____
_____

With a torch, whose flame
Is the imprisoned lightning, and her name
Mother of Exiles.

_____
_____
_____
_____

From her beacon-hand
Glows world-wide welcome;

Semitic feelings even among her friends.

Comprehension and Discussion Questions

- Why does Lazarus say the Statue of Liberty has a "beacon-hand"? *The statue carries a torch in her right hand.*

- Do you think Lazarus might have had a special understanding of these lines, since she came from a Jewish family? *Answers will vary.*

- When you welcome someone to your home, or into your school, how do you do it? *Smiling, showing them around, helping them to feel at home.*

- How do you feel when you are "welcome" somewhere? *Happy, at ease, comfortable.*

Notes: _____

_____
_____
_____
_____
_____
_____
_____
_____
_____
_____
_____
_____
_____
_____
_____
_____

Supplementary Information

- Like all Americans, Lazarus came from an immigrant family. Her family, Sephardic Jews (from Spain and Portugal), had long settled in New York and was part of the Jewish upper class.

- Lazarus' father wished for his seven children to become part of Christian society. The family's social and business circle included the Vanderbilts and the Astors. Despite her family's attempt to assimilate, Lazarus wrote in a letter that she was "perfectly conscious" of anti-

Supplementary Information

- In contrast to the "brazen" Colossus of Rhodes, the Statue of Liberty has "mild eyes."
- The Statue of Liberty faces seaward — symbolically facing France. The New York skyline is not visible from the observation area in the crown.
- The plaque on the Statue of Liberty pedestal mistakenly omits the comma after the word "keep."

Comprehension and Discussion Questions

- The statue's eyes "command" the harbor. Do you think this means the statue faces New York, or that it faces toward the sea? *The statue faces the sea. It looks at France; the statue was a gift from that country.*
- What are the "twin cities" framing the harbor? *New York City, and Brooklyn, New York.*
- Why does the statue have "silent lips"? *The Statue of Liberty cannot speak, but it communicates through its face, its structure, and its symbolism.*
- What does the Statue of Liberty say to "ancient lands"? *To keep their storied pomp.*
- What does that mean? *Ancient lands can keep all their old traditions and stories of grandeur.*

Notes: _____

_____

_____

_____

Her mild eyes command
The air-bridged harbor that twin cities frame.
"Keep, ancient lands, your storied pomp!" cries she
With silent lips.

"Give me your tired, your poor,
Your huddled masses yearning to breathe free,
The wretched refuse of your teeming shore.
Send these, the homeless, tempest-tost to me,

Supplementary Information

- The Statue of Liberty is "speaking" in these lines of the poem.
- These are the most-often quoted lines from *The New Colossus*.
- The Statue of Liberty has broken shackles at its feet, representing freedom from oppression.

Comprehension and Discussion Questions

- What does the Statue of Liberty ask for in these lines? *Send me the people who are very tired and longing for freedom. I will take care of them and give them a home.*

- What kinds of pictures of immigrants does Lazarus paint with these lines? *Immigrants are exhausted; they only have each other (as they are huddled together); they want freedom; they have been through hard times to make it to America.*

- A tempest is a storm. What do you think Lazarus means by "tempest-tost"? *Immigrants may have faced storms on the sea during their voyages to America, but she could also mean the "stormy" past of immigrants — whatever struggles they went through in their homelands that led them to want to come to America.*

Notes: _____

_____
_____
_____
_____
_____
_____
_____
_____
_____
_____
_____
_____

Supplementary Information

- James Russell Lowell wrote to Lazarus, "your sonnet gives its subject a *raison d'etre*."
- A sonnet is a type of 14-line poem. *The New Colossus* has 14 lines.
- Sixteen years after Lazarus' death in 1887, a plaque with her poem was added to the pedestal of the Statue of Liberty.
- The Statue of Liberty does not open the door, merely lifts her lamp beside it. Therefore, the light of liberty enlightens the world. It shows people the door. But they must open and enter it themselves.

Comprehension and Discussion Questions

- Who is saying "I lift my lamp beside the golden door!"? *The Statue of Liberty is speaking these lines in the poem.*
- Where does the golden door lead? *Liberty, America.*
- Why did Lazarus describe the door as "golden"? What does that color make you think of? *Golden could refer to a glorious sunrise, valuable gold, treasure, riches, the light of her torch, the light of liberty.*
- How do you think Lazarus wanted these lines to make people feel? *Hopeful, excited, welcome, proud of America.*

Notes: _____
_____
_____
_____
_____

I lift my lamp beside the golden door!"

48

_____
_____
_____
_____

The New Colossus

Not like the brazen giant of Greek fame,

With conquering limbs astride from land to land;

Here at our sea-washed, sunset gates shall stand

A mighty woman with a torch, whose flame

Is the imprisoned lightning, and her name

Mother of Exiles. From her beacon-hand

Glows world-wide welcome; her mild eyes command

The air-bridged harbor that twin cities frame.

"Keep, ancient lands, your storied pomp!" cries she

With silent lips. "Give me your tired, your poor,

Your huddled masses yearning to breathe free,

The wretched refuse of your teeming shore.

Send these, the homeless, tempest-tost to me,

I lift my lamp beside the golden door!"

Name: _____ Date: _____

Wrap-up Discussion Questions

- Why do you think Emma Lazarus began her poem by comparing the Statue of Liberty to an ancient Greek statue?

- Is the Statue of Liberty a good symbol for America?

- When a writer "paints a picture" in your mind using words, that is called imagery. What examples of imagery can you find in the poem?

- Which parts of the poem do you think you will remember the most?

- If this poem were set to music, what kind of music would it be?

Teaching Suggestions

Activity I: Close Reading

Separate the class into pairs or trios and give each group a slip of paper with an excerpt from *The New Colossus* (**Graphic Organizer A**). Have them put the sentence(s) in their own words. After a few moments, reconvene the class and distribute complete copies of **Handout A** to each student. Have groups read their paraphrases in turn, and discuss each as a class and decide if it is a faithful and complete paraphrase. Have students complete the chart on **Handout A** with the class paraphrases. When all slips are completed, read the original version of *The New Colossus* aloud and discuss how the class version compared with the original.

Activity II: Analysis

1. Have students choose their favorite image from *The New Colossus*. Have them write the words in the center of a piece of paper and draw a circle around it. Then have them create a word web of all the other images or ideas the words remind them of. They might choose to begin with "brazen giant," "conquering limbs," "sunset gates," "imprisoned lightning," etc.

2. Post word webs around the room and give students a chance to view them all. Then reconvene the class for a large group discussion. Did these words sound good together? How did these images make them feel? Which are the most memorable to them? Which are the most forgettable? Why?

Activity III: Creative Writing

Ask students to imagine that they have been asked to design a new Statue of Liberty to represent the United States and its promise of liberty. Have students work in groups to design a new statue. They should draw or paint their statue on poster board. Then ask them to imagine they have been asked, as Emma Lazarus was, to write a poem about their new Statue of Liberty. Have them write a six- to eight-line poem. It does not have to rhyme.

Activity IV: Application

Have students write a six- to eight-line poem about an object in their life they believe is beautiful and/or meaningful. Encourage students to choose something that makes them feel inspired. Then have students share their poems with the class, along with a photograph of the subject (or the subject itself, if it can be brought to class).

Activity V: Evaluation

Have students interview three people: one should be a peer, one should be a parent/guardian, and one should be a grandparent or someone of their grandparents' age. Have students begin the interview by reading Lazarus' poem aloud to their interviewee. They should then use **Handout B** to guide the interview and record their conversations.

Name: _____ Date: _____

Graphic Organizer A

Not like the brazen giant of Greek fame, With conquering limbs astride from land to land;	*Put this passage in your own words:*
Here at our sea-washed, sunset gates shall stand A mighty woman	*Put this passage in your own words:*
With a torch, whose flame Is the imprisoned lightning, and her name Mother of Exiles.	*Put this passage in your own words:*
From her beacon-hand Glows world-wide welcome;	*Put this passage in your own words:*
Her mild eyes command The air-bridged harbor that twin cities frame. "Keep, ancient lands, your storied pomp!" cries she With silent lips,	*Put this passage in your own words:*
"Give me your tired, your poor, Your huddled masses yearning to breathe free, The wretched refuse of your teeming shore. Send these, the homeless, tempest-tost to me,	*Put this passage in your own words:*
I lift my lamp beside the golden door!"	*Put this passage in your own words:*

AIHE American Institute for History Education

© 2010 American Institute for History Education

Handout B: Interview

Not like the brazen giant of Greek fame, With conquering limbs astride from land to land; Here at our sea-washed, sunset gates shall stand A mighty woman with a torch, whose flame Is the imprisoned lightning, and her name Mother of Exiles. From her beacon-hand Glows world-wide welcome; her mild eyes command The air-bridged harbor that twin cities frame. "Keep, ancient lands, your storied pomp!" cries she With silent lips. "Give me your tired, your poor, Your huddled masses yearning to breathe free, The wretched refuse of your teeming shore. Send these, the homeless, tempest-tost to me, I lift my lamp beside the golden door!"

Question	Friend's Answer	Parent's Answer	Grandparent's Answer	My Thoughts
Who do you think this poem is about?				
What do you think is "beside the golden door!"?				
Why is the Statue of Liberty important in American history?				